WHY DO I SNEEZE?

✦ and other questions about breathing ✦

Heinemann
LIBRARY

Angela Royston

www.heinemann.co.uk/library
Visit our website to find out more information about **Heinemann Library** books.

To order:
 Phone 44 (0) 1865 888066
 Send a fax to 44 (0) 1865 314091
 Visit the Heinemann Bookshop at www.heinemann.co.uk/library to browse our catalogue and order online.

First published in Great Britain by Heinemann Library, Halley Court, Jordan Hill, Oxford OX2 8EJ, a division of Reed Educational and Professional Publishing Ltd. Heinemann is a registered trademark of Reed Educational & Professional Publishing Limited.

OXFORD MELBOURNE AUCKLAND JOHANNESBURG BLANTYRE
GABORONE IBADAN PORTSMOUTH NH (USA) CHICAGO

Designed by Joanna Sapwell and StoryBooks
Illustrations by Nick Hawken
Originated by Ambassador Litho Ltd
Printed in China by South China Printing Company

ISBN 0 431 11070 0
06 05 04 03 02
10 9 8 7 6 5 4 3 2 1

British Library Cataloguing in Publication Data
    Royston, Angela
    Why do I sneeze?.– (Body matters)
    1. Sneezing – Juvenile literature
    I.Title
    612.8'6

Acknowledgements
The Publishers would like to thank the following for permission to reproduce photographs:
Gareth Boden: 5, 7, 8, 9, 15, 23, 28; Popperfoto: 27; Powerstock Zefa: 10, 24; Robert Harding: 11; Science Photo Library: 16, 17, 18, 19, 21, 22, 25, 26; Stone: 6.

Cover photograph reproduced with permission of Science Photo Library/Damien Lovegrove.

Our thanks to Anne Long for her help in the preparation of this book.

Every effort has been made to contact copyright holders of any material reproduced in this book. Any omissions will be rectified in subsequent printings if notice is given to the Publisher.

CONTENTS

Words printed in **bold letters like these** are explained in the Glossary.

WHAT HAPPENS WHEN I BREATHE?

When you breathe in, oxygen from the air passes into your lungs and then into your blood. Air containing carbon dioxide leaves your body when you breathe out.

Oxygen is essential for all living things, including humans, animals, plants and even **bacteria**. When you breathe in, air – a mixture of invisible gases that includes oxygen – is pulled through your nose or mouth, down the **trachea** (windpipe), to your lungs.

Inside the lungs

The trachea is a wide, tough tube that looks a bit like a vacuum cleaner tube. It divides into two **bronchial tubes**, one for each lung. The bronchial tubes split into many smaller, narrower tubes. At the end of each narrow tube is a cluster of air sacs with lots of tiny **blood vessels** flowing around them. The air sacs

trachea

lung

heart

bronchial tube

blood vessels

alveoli

are called alveoli and each one is like a tiny balloon. As each fills with air, oxygen from the air passes through its thin wall into the blood.

How the body uses oxygen

Blood carries oxygen to every **cell** in your body, including the millions of cells that make up your brain, muscles and bones. Every cell needs energy to do its job. It gets the energy by using oxygen to burn glucose (sugar) from your food. This produces waste, including carbon dioxide that is transported in the blood until it passes through the walls of the alveoli and joins the air in the lungs. You breathe out this stale air.

The air you breathe out contains some water vapour. If you breathe onto a cold mirror, the water forms a mist on the glass.

WHY CAN'T I HOLD MY BREATH FOR LONG?

You can survive for a few days without water and a few weeks without food, but you cannot survive for more than a few minutes without **oxygen**. You do not have to think about breathing — your body does it automatically. When you hold your breath, the amount of oxygen in your blood drops, and your body desperately wants to breathe in more air. Soon you are forced to breathe in.

Healthy lungs

Some people can hold their breath for longer than other people. Swimmers and other athletes have healthy lungs and good breathing muscles. When they breathe in, the air reaches more of their alveoli and so their bodies take in more oxygen with each breath. This means that they can last longer before they have to breathe again.

This girl is gasping for air. She has been holding her breath to swim as far as she can underwater.

Yawning

You often yawn when you are tired or when you are in a stuffy room. Yawning makes you take in a deep breath of air. This provides the brain with extra oxygen to make you more alert.

When your brain is not getting enough oxygen, you begin to feel drowsy. Yawning pulls more air, and so more oxygen, into your lungs.

Fainting

The brain needs a lot of oxygen to stay alert. If the brain does not get enough oxygen, you may faint. This means that you lose consciousness. If you feel faint or dizzy, bend forward and put your head between your knees. This brings more blood and therefore more oxygen to your brain.

WHY DO I SNEEZE?

Sneezing clears the inside of your nose of something that is irritating it. Air is made up of gases but it also contains dust, **germs** and other tiny specks that are mostly too small to see. When you breathe in, some of these tiny specks are pulled into your nose.

Jet of air

The delicate skin inside your nose is protected by a layer of **mucus** that traps dirt and germs. Sometimes a particular speck irritates the lining of your nose, making it itch and tingle. This triggers a sneeze. A strong jet of air rushes from the lungs, down the nostrils, and sweeps mucus and any irritating specks out of the nose.

Grains of pepper make many people sneeze if they breathe them in. Sneezing helps to sweep the grains out of the nose.

Other causes of sneezing

Often, one of the first signs of a cold is sneezing. Colds and flu are caused by germs that you breathe in. If some of these germs get stuck in the lining of your nostrils, you automatically sneeze to clear them away. This helps to get rid of the germs, but make sure that you sneeze into a tissue. Otherwise you may pass the germs to the people around you. Some people are **allergic** to things they breathe in, such as pollen or tiny specks of dust. Their bodies think the specks are harmful germs and they sneeze.

THINGS THAT MIGHT MAKE YOU SNEEZE:

- pepper
- dust
- sunlight
- germs
- pollen, cat hair, mould or other cause of allergy.

When you sneeze air rushes down your nose at 110 kilometres per hour (70 miles per hour) – as fast as a car on the motorway – or even faster.

WHY DO I PUFF AND PANT?

The fastest sprinters can run 100 metres on one breath of air. At the end of the race, however, they are gasping for air.

You puff and pant when your body is desperate for **oxygen**. Panting makes you breathe faster and take in more air with each breath. This quickly provides your body with a large amount of oxygen. As more oxygen gets into your blood, your breathing becomes calmer again.

Exercise

When you breathe normally you only empty and fill about a tenth of your lungs with each breath. When you exercise you breathe deeper and take in more air. Exercise that uses a lot of energy makes you puff and pant. Then you take in about fifteen times the amount of air.

Muscles use oxygen

Exercise means that your muscles are moving your bones. Muscles get their energy by using oxygen to burn glucose (sugar). Glucose comes from food and is brought to the muscles in the blood. The harder the muscles work, the more energy – and so the more oxygen – they need.

Red blood cells

Oxygen is carried in the blood by red blood **cells**. When oxygen becomes attached to a red cell, the cell becomes a brighter colour of red. Blood that is low in oxygen is a dark red. About a quarter of the oxygen you breathe in enters your blood. Puffing and panting help to attach more oxygen to more red blood cells.

PANTING INCREASES SUPPLY OF OXYGEN

When an adult is resting they breathe in less than 0.5 litres with every breath and about 6 litres a minute. When they are sprinting, they breathe in about 90 litres of air a minute – 15 times as much as usual.

These children are running as fast as they can. If they keep running like this, they will soon be puffing and panting.

Heart-beat

Exercise that makes you puff and pant also makes your heart beat faster. You can often feel it thudding in your chest. The heart is a pump that pushes blood through the **arteries** and around your body. The faster it beats, the faster blood passes through your lungs and the faster it picks up **oxygen** to take it to your muscles.

The heart pumps blood to the lungs where it picks up oxygen. The blood returns to the heart which then pumps it around the body.

Fit and healthy

Regular exercise makes your muscles, heart and lungs work better. The more you exercise the stronger your muscles become. The heart is a muscle and exercise makes it stronger too. A strong heart pushes more blood through the arteries with every beat. Healthy lungs take in more oxygen from the air with every breath.

lung

lung

right side of heart pumps blood to lungs

left side of heart pumps blood to body

vein takes blood back to heart

artery

CHILDREN'S LUNGS

A 10-year-old child's lungs hold about 3 litres of air. Children tend to breathe faster than adults – about 20 times a minute compared to about 15 times a minute for an adult.

When your heart, lungs and muscles are fit, you can do much more exercise before you begin to puff and pant.

Poor breathing

Unfit people, who do not exercise much, take in only a small amount of air with each breath. They easily begin to puff and pant. People who are overweight also become breathless quickly. Smoking tobacco damages the lungs and so heavy smokers quickly become out of breath. Illnesses, such as **bronchitis**, also affect how well people can breathe.

This woman is climbing a hill. She has to rest every few steps, so she does not become breathless.

WHAT ARE HICCUPS?

Hiccups occur when air is suddenly and unexpectedly jerked into your lungs. When you cough, you know that you are going to push air out, but a hiccup often takes you by surprise. Hiccups are caused by a flat sheet of muscle called the diaphragm. It lies underneath your lungs and is the main muscle that you use to breathe in and out.

Your lungs expand and contract as you breathe in and out. The movement is controlled by the diaphragm. A hiccup is caused by a twitch in the diaphragm.

Breathing in and out

Lungs have no muscles of their own. Instead the diaphragm and the muscles between your ribs control your breathing. To breathe in, the diaphragm moves down and the ribs move up and out. This creates space in your chest that is filled by air being pulled into your lungs. To breathe out, the diaphragm moves up and the ribs move in. This squeezes air out of the lungs.

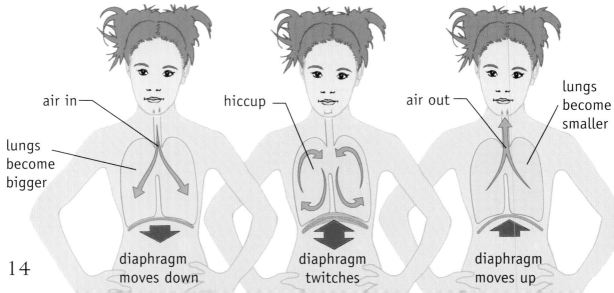

air in

hiccup

air out

lungs become smaller

lungs become bigger

14

diaphragm moves down

diaphragm twitches

diaphragm moves up

Hiccups

You get hiccups when your diaphragm twitches or jerks downwards. This pulls in a gasp of air. At the same time the top of the **trachea** snaps shut. The air is then forced through the **larynx**, causing the 'hic' sound. Different things can cause hiccups, such as eating lots of fresh bread or spicy food. Most bouts of hiccups last only a few minutes, but some unlucky people can suffer for days.

This boy is trying to stop his hiccups. Different people have different ways of curing hiccups. You have to find which way works for you.

POSSIBLE HICCUP CURES:

- holding your breath
- drinking a cup of water from the far side of the cup
- breathing in and out of a paper bag
- sucking sugar.

WHAT HAPPENS WHEN I BREATHE POLLUTED AIR?

Polluted air is air that contains specks of dirt, or chemicals from factories, car exhausts and other sources. Large specks of dirt might make you sneeze but smaller specks pass through your nose or mouth and into your lungs.

The tiny hairs in your breathing tubes look like this under a microscope. They catch dirt and **germs** and push them back along the tubes out of the lungs.

Protecting the lungs

The **bronchial tubes** and the tubes in your lungs are protected by **mucus** and by very fine hairs. The hairs and mucus trap dust and specks that get into your lungs. The hairs waft backwards and forwards to push the mucus and the specks out of the lungs.

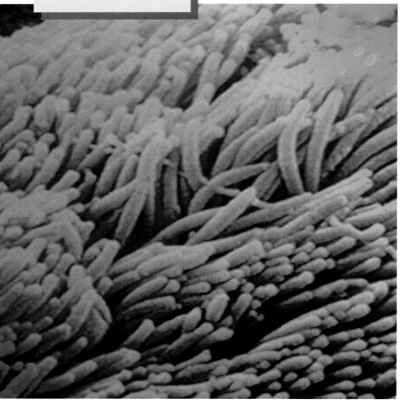

Coughing

If the tubes become clogged with mucus, you automatically cough to clear them. Coughing forces a blast of air through the tubes, **trachea** and throat to clear them.

Damaging chemicals

Some chemicals stay in the lungs and can damage them. They may irritate the lining of the tubes and make breathing more difficult. If you suffer from **asthma** or **bronchitis**, it is already difficult to breathe and air pollution makes it worse. Some chemicals can even cause cancer of the lungs.

Ozone

The gas ozone is produced at ground level when sunlight acts on the exhaust fumes of cars, lorries and other traffic. Breathing air with a lot of ozone can give you a sore throat.

When sunlight combines with traffic fumes it produces ozone and a kind of fog called photochemical smog. It can make your throat sore and irritate your lungs.

THINGS THAT CAUSE AIR POLLUTION:

Outside –
- exhaust fumes from traffic
- waste gases from power stations, oil refineries, factories and chimneys
- chemical sprays on crops.

Inside –
- cleaning materials
- household pest sprays
- paint and glue sprays.

Smoking tobacco

Tobacco smoke is one of the most dangerous things that pollute the air. Tobacco smoke contains the gas carbon monoxide and more than 4000 different chemicals, including the poisons arsenic, hydrogen cyanide and formaldehyde. Smokers also take in two other damaging substances – tar and nicotine.

Carbon monoxide

Carbon monoxide passes through the lungs into the blood. It attaches itself to red blood **cells** and so takes the place of **oxygen** in the blood. This means that there is less oxygen to supply the brain, heart and other parts of the body.

The air in this room is polluted with cigarette smoke. Breathing in other people's cigarette smoke is called 'passive smoking'. It can cause lung cancer and other diseases.

Damaging the lungs

Smokers breathe hot gases and chemicals straight into their lungs. The smoke burns their throat and damages the fine hairs and delicate lining of their breathing tubes. The body makes extra **mucus** to try to get rid of the smoke, but their damaged lungs cannot clear the mucus so smokers often develop a 'smoker's cough'.

Tar and nicotine

Tobacco smoke contains black, sticky tar, rather like the tar that is laid on the roads. Over time, it clogs the lungs and stops them from working properly. Nicotine is an addictive drug. This means that people who smoke crave the nicotine and need it for their bodies to work normally.

The healthy lungs on the left belonged to a non-smoker. Those on the right belonged to a smoker and are clearly dirty and damaged.

SOME DISEASES CAUSED BY SMOKING:

- bronchitis
- smoker's cough
- emphysema
- lung cancer
- throat and mouth cancer

WHY DOES A COLD MAKE MY NOSE BLOCKED?

The inside of the nose. Each nostril leads to a nasal passage filled with three shelves of bone. When you have a cold, these passageways become clogged with mucus.

Your nose is much bigger than it looks from the outside. Each nostril leads to a passageway which contains three shelves of bone. These shelves are lined with **mucus**. When you have a cold, your nose makes extra mucus. The mucus may become so thick it blocks your nose and makes it harder to breathe.

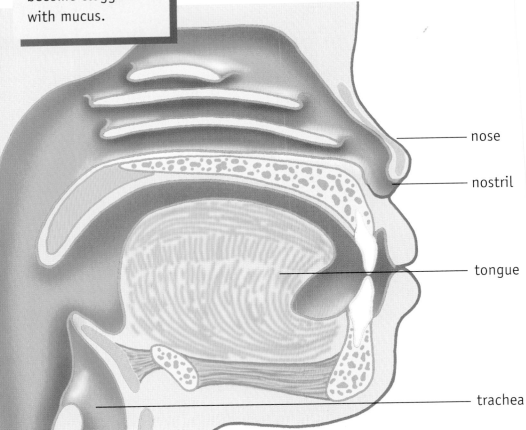

nose

nostril

tongue

trachea

Inflamed and swollen

When you breathe in cold **germs**, they lodge in your throat or nose. Germs that lodge in your throat make it red and sore. When germs stick in your nose, the passageways at the back of your nose become swollen. Your body makes extra mucus to wash the germs away, but the swelling stops the mucus escaping.

Fighting germs

Most germs are killed by your body before they have a chance to multiply. Mucus and saliva are antiseptic (they help to kill germs), but any germs that survive can multiply quickly. Blood contains white blood **cells**. Their job is to destroy germs. The blood also makes **antibodies** that attack germs.

Getting rid of mucus

Mucus washes away some of the germs. It also washes away dead germs, killed by white blood cells and by antibodies. You get rid of the extra mucus when you blow your nose. Sometimes the mucus becomes so thick with germs it clogs your nostrils. Then you have to breathe through your mouth.

A cold makes your nose run with extra mucus. Even if you blow your nose, the passageways soon fill with more mucus.

Cold viruses

Colds are caused by a **virus**. A virus is a particular kind of germ and there are over 200 different kinds that cause colds. When you have a cold, your body may be invaded by more than one cold virus. One common cold virus is yellow, another one is blue. If your cold is caused by both, the colours of the viruses combine to turn your **mucus** green!

This is what one kind of cold germ looks like under a microscope. Several different viruses can cause a cold.

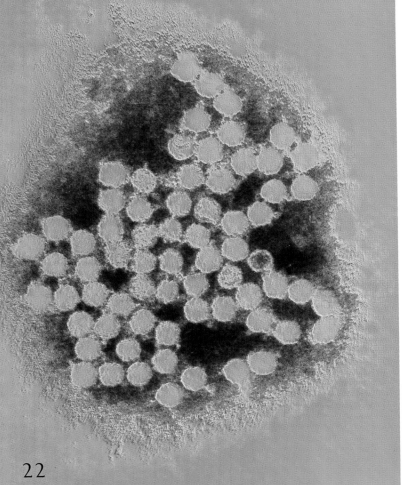

Coughs

Some of the mucus from the nose drains down the throat into the **bronchial tubes**. Colds are often followed by coughs as your body works to clear all the breathing tubes. Sometimes the bronchial tubes become infected by **bacteria** after a cold. Then you suffer from a chest infection. There is no cure for a virus, but the doctor can give you medicine to cure an infection caused by bacteria.

Sinuses

Sinuses are spaces in the bones of the head and face. They make your skull lighter and so make it easier for you to hold your head up. These hollows are lined with mucus and are normally filled with air. The mucus drains into the nose.

Sinusitis

When you have a cold, the infection can spread into one or more of the sinuses. Then the sinuses become inflamed and the entrance to the nose becomes blocked. The mucus is trapped in the sinus. This can make you feel dizzy and give you a painful headache. It can also add to your blocked nose.

Coughing helps to clear your bronchial tubes. Always cover your mouth when you cough. If you don't you may spread germs to other people.

WHAT MAKES SOME PEOPLE WHEEZE?

People who have **asthma** often wheeze when they breathe. The tubes in their lungs are swollen and narrower than other people's. During an asthma attack the tubes close up and become even narrower. This makes breathing very difficult, particularly breathing out. There is often a whistling sound as they breathe in and a wheezing sound as they breathe out. Asthma is most common among children.

Allergies often run in families. The girl in this photo has asthma, her mother has hayfever, her brother has eczema and her father has asthma.

Causes of asthma

The most common cause of asthma is an allergy to something such as house dust, pollen or certain foods. Contact with the thing a person is **allergic** to sets off an asthma attack. An attack can also be triggered by worry or excitement.

An asthma attack

One of the first signs that an attack is about to happen is a feeling of tightness in the chest. The muscles in the **bronchial tubes** tighten up and the lining of the tubes makes extra **mucus**. Together these make the tubes so narrow it is very difficult for air to pass through them. The person becomes breathless and gasps for air, and is unable to breathe properly. Being unable to stop coughing is another early sign of an attack. An attack may last for a few minutes, or a few hours or even several days.

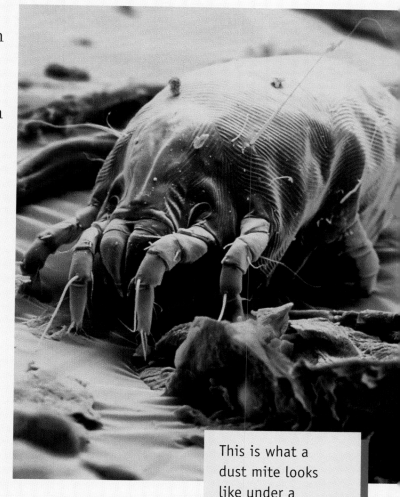

This is what a dust mite looks like under a microscope. Dust mites are too small to see unless they are magnified, but they are a common cause of asthma.

THINGS THAT MAY TRIGGER AN ASTHMA ATTACK:

- tobacco smoke
- pollen
- cold air
- coughs and colds
- pets
- house dust
- exercise
- aspirin

Medicines

There is no cure for **asthma**, but there are medicines that help to control it. Most people with asthma have medicines that they breathe in through an **inhaler**. These drugs make the muscles of the airways relax and open. One medicine helps to relieve an attack. It is taken when the person feels an attack coming on.

Another medicine helps to prevent an attack happening. It has to be inhaled (breathed in) every day.

This girl is inhaling a drug that will help to prevent her from getting a severe asthma attack.

Treating asthma

An asthma attack can be frightening both for the person having it and for the people with them. It is important that the person with asthma sits down and that everyone stays calm. The person suffering the attack tries to cough the sticky **mucus** up from their lungs.

Once they have coughed mucus out of their lungs, the attack often begins to pass. This makes coughing easier. If the attack does not ease quickly then you should get medical help.

A normal life

If people with asthma take their medicines, they can do most of the things other people do. They can join in with games and other exercise. Most children who suffer from asthma find that their attacks become milder and less frequent as they reach their teens. About half of all children who have asthma grow out of the condition completely.

Some adults continue to suffer from asthma. Tom Dolan is an Olympic athlete who also has asthma.

WHY DO I HAVE TO STOP TALKING TO BREATHE IN?

You can only talk as you breathe out. Air from your lungs is pushed through the **larynx** in your throat to produce sound. It does not work when you breathe in! The larynx contains two bands of skin called the vocal cords. They vibrate when air passes between them. Muscles stretch and relax the bands to produce different notes. The more relaxed the vocal cords, the lower the note.

You make sounds in your larynx in your throat. If you hold your hand over your throat as you hum, you will feel the voice box vibrate as you make the noise.

Talking and shouting

The larynx produces the note, but you move your lips, tongue and teeth to make the many different sounds that make up speech. You cannot talk with your mouth shut! To talk louder you have to push a greater amount of air out of your lungs. Before you shout, you need to take in a deep breath of air.

BODY MAP

nose

sinuses

trachea

lungs

bronchial tube

alveoli

GLOSSARY

allergic   when the body reacts to something as if it were a germ, even though that thing is harmless to most people

antibodies   cells carried in the blood that attack particular bacteria and viruses

arteries   tubes that blood flows along from the heart to different parts of the body

asthma   condition in which the breathing tubes become inflamed and narrower than usual. This makes it difficult to breathe air into and out of the lungs.

bacteria   tiny living things. Some kinds of bacteria are germs that cause disease.

blood vessels   tubes through which blood moves around the body

bronchial tubes   tubes that join the trachea to the lungs

bronchitis   when the bronchial tubes become inflamed, causing a deep cough

cell   the smallest building block of living things. The body has many kinds of cells, including nasal cells, lung cells and blood cells.

germs   tiny forms of life that can make you ill

inhaler   equipment used to take medicine that must be breathed in

larynx   the voice box, that is, the part of the trachea that contains the vocal cords

mucus   slime that coats the inside of parts of the body, including the nose and bronchial tubes

oxygen   a gas that living things need to breathe in to survive

trachea   the tube that connects the throat to the bronchial tubes

virus   a kind of germ that is even smaller than all kinds of bacteria

FURTHER READING

Body Works: Breathing, Paul Bennett, 1998, Belitha Press

The Human Machine: The Power Pack, Sarah Angliss, 2000, Belitha Press

Your Body: Breathing, A. Sandeman, 2000, Franklin Watts

INDEX

Titles in the *Body Matters* series include:

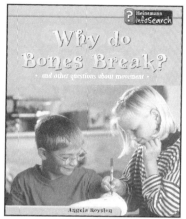

Hardback   0431 11075 1

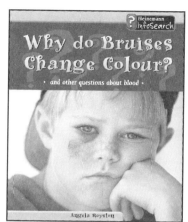

Hardback   0431 11073 5

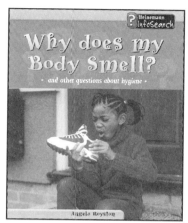

Hardback   0431 11077 8

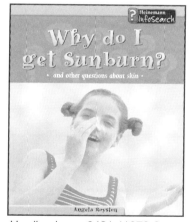

Hardback   0431 11078 6

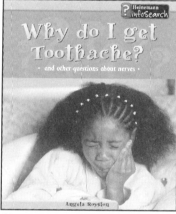

Hardback   0431 11076 X

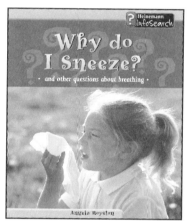

Hardback   0431 11070 0

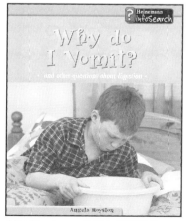

Hardback   0431 11072 7

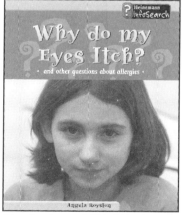

Hardback   0431 11071 9

Find out about the other titles in this series on our website www.heinemann.co.uk/library